YOU

ARE

NOT

YOUR

MISTAKES

JOTTER

Date:

You are not your mistakes jotter

Date:

Date:

Date:

You are not your mistakes jotter

Date:

Date:

You are not your mistakes jotter

Date:

Date:

Date:

Date:

Date:

You are not your mistakes jotter

Date:

You are not your mistakes jotter

Date:

You are not your mistakes jotter

Date:

You are not your mistakes jotter

Date:

Date:

Date:

Date:

Date:

Date:

Date:

You are not your mistakes jotter

Date:

Date:

Date:

You are not your mistakes jotter

Date:

Date:

Date:

Date:

Date:

Date:

You are not your mistakes jotter

Date:

Date:

You are not your mistakes jotter

Date:

You are not your mistakes jotter

Date:

Date:

Date:

You are not your mistakes jotter

Date:

Date:

Date:

You are not your mistakes jotter

Date:

Date:

You are not your mistakes jotter

Date:

Date:

You are not your mistakes jotter

Date:

Date:

Date:

Date:

Date:

Date:

You are not your mistakes jotter

Date:

You are not your mistakes jotter

Date:

Date:

You are not your mistakes jotter

Date:

You are not your mistakes jotter

Date:

You are not your mistakes jotter